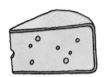   

Children have always been fascinated by nursery rhymes and for good reason! The sheer silliness of them is irresistible. But there is an important learning aspect to nursery rhymes as well. They introduce the delight and enchantment of books to the very youngest child and now, with THE REAL MOTHER GOOSE® PICTURE WORD RHYMES, they can also begin to teach children to read!

In each rhyme, certain words have been replaced with pictures. Suddenly, "Hey, diddle diddle! The cat and the fiddle" becomes " diddle, diddle! The and the ." As you go through each rhyme with your child, let them interpret the pictures so that they can read along with you. The fun of the familiar rhyme expands into the fun of reading!

Each picture used in the rhyme is also shown at the bottom of the page. The first word to appear under that picture shows the correct spelling of the picture. For example, underneath appears "hay." Sometimes there is a second word in parentheses. It shows the correct spelling for the word the picture replaces in the rhyme –(hey). This glossary helps your child to understand the connection of words to symbols and introduces them to the fact that some words sound alike but are spelled differently and have different meanings.

Reading and learning can bring a lifetime of pleasure. . .and it all begins with nursery rhymes!

Copyright © 1916, 1944, 1987 Checkerboard Press,
a division of Macmillan, Inc.
All rights reserved. Printed in Singapore
Library of Congress Catalog Card Number: 87-42841

398.8
MOT

ISBN 0–516–09893–4   OCLC: 17892156

CHECKERBOARD PRESS and colophon,
THE REAL MOTHER GOOSE® and the
checkerboard cover design are trademarks
of Macmillan, Inc.

THE REAL
MOTHER GOOSE®
PICTURE WORD
RHYMES

Illustrated by
Blanche Fisher Wright

CHILDRENS PRESS CHOICE

A Checkerboard Press/Macmillan title selected for educational distribution.

eye
(I)

bread

cheese

shelf

rats

WHEN

When 👁 was a bachelor
👁 lived by myself;
And all the 🍞 and 🧀
👁 got 👁 laid up on the 🪑.
The 🐀 and the 🐭
They made such a strife,
👁 was forced 2 go 2 London
2 buy me a wife.
The ✖ were 🧵 bad,
And the lanes were 🧵 narrow,
👁 was forced 2 bring my wife home
In a 🛒. The 🛒 broke,
And my wife had a fall;
Down came 🛒,
Little wife and all.

 mice    two (to)    streets    sew (so)    wheelbarrow

stairs

lady

GOOSEY, GOOSEY, GANDER

Goosey, goosey, gander,
    Whither dost thou wander?
Up ![stairs] and down ![stairs]
    And in my ![lady] 's chamber.
There  met an old ![man]
    Who wouldn't say his prayers;
 took him by the left ![leg],
    And threw him down the ![stairs].

---

eye   man   leg

clock

school

two

THE CLOCK

There's a neat little 🕐,
　　In the 🏫 room it stands,
And it points to the time
　　With its **2** little 🖐🖐.
And may we, like the 🕐,
　　🔑+p a 🙂 clean and bright,
With 🖐🖐 ever ready
　　To do what is right.

hands

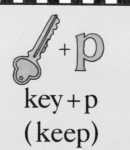

key+p
(keep)

face

jack
(Jack)

JACK

 nimble,
quick,
jump over
the .

bee
(be)

candle + stick
(candlestick)

wind

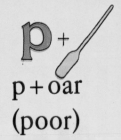
p + oar
(poor)

robin

THE ROBIN

The north (wind) doth blow,
  And we shall have snow,
And what will p+(oar)(robin) do then,
   p+(oar) thing?
He'll sit in a (barn),
  And (key)+p himself warm,
And hide his (head) under his (wing),
   p+(oar) thing!

barn

key + p
(keep)

head

wing

four
(for)

supper

bread

LITTLE TOM TUCKER

Little Tom Tucker
    Sings **4** his .
What shall he eat?
    White 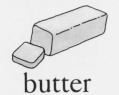 and .
How will he cut it
    Without e'er a ?
How will he  married
    Without e'er a wife?

butter

knife

bee
(be)

queen

hearts

tarts

king

THE TARTS

The 👑 of 💕,
She made some 🥧,
All on a summer's day;
The Knave of 💕,
He stole the 🥧,
And took them clean away.
The 👑 of 💕
Called **4** the 🥧,
And beat the Knave full **s**+🥄;
The Knave of 💕
Brought 🧒 the 🥧,
And vowed he'd **st**+🐍 no **m**+🥄.

s+ 🥄	4	🧒	st+ 🐍	m+ 🥄
s+oar (sore)	four (for)	back	st+eel (steal)	m+oar (more)

pumpkin

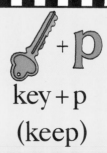
key + p
(keep)

THE PUMPKIN-EATER

Peter, Peter,
-eater,
Had a wife and
couldn't +p her:
He put her in
a ,
And there he kept her
very  .

 shell    well

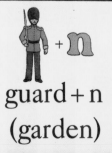

guard + n
(garden)

bells

MARY, MARY, QUITE CONTRARY

Mary, Mary, quite contrary,
How does your +n grow?
Silver 🔔🔔 and cockle- ,
And pretty 👭 all of a row.

shells

maids

fly

house

fire

LADYBIRD

Ladybird, ladybird,
      away home!
Your 🏠 is on 🔥,
     your children all gone,
All but **1**,
     and her name is Ann,
And she crept under
     the 🍨 🍳.

one

pudding

pan

cock

m + eye
(my)

shoe

fiddle + sti
(fiddlestic

COCK-A-DOODLE-DO!

🐔-a-doodle-do!
 M + 👁 dame has lost her 👠,
M + 👁 master's lost his 🎻 + 🎵,
And 👃 🪢 what 2 do.
🐓-a-doodle-do!
 What is m + 👁 dame 2 do?
Till master finds his 🎻 + 🎵,
 She'll d + 🐜 without her 👠.

nose	knot	two	d + ants
knows)	(not)	(to)	(dance)

woman

basket

h + eye
(high)

moon

four
(for)

arm

OLD WOMAN, OLD WOMAN

There was an old tossed in
a ,
Seventeen times as h+ as the
;
But where she was going no mortal
could tell,
4 under her she carried a
.
"Old , old , old
," said I,
"Whither, oh whither, oh whither
h+?"
"2 sweep the +s from the sk+ ;
And I'll with you by-and-by."

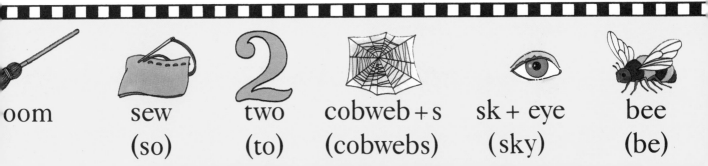

oom   sew   two   cobweb+s   sk+eye   bee
                 (so)   (to)   (cobwebs)   (sky)   (be)

 pocket

 birds

 pie

 knot
(not)

 dish

 kin

SING A SONG OF SIXPENCE

Sing a song of sixpence,
    a (shirt) full of rye,
Four-and-twenty black (birds)
    baked in a (pie)!
When the (pie) was opened
    The (bird) began to sing;
Was (that) that a dainty (dish)
    To set before the (king)?
The (king) was in his counting-house,
    Counting out his (money);
The (queen) was in the parlor,
    Eating (bread) and honey.
The (maid) was in the (guard)+n,
    Hanging out the clothes;
When down came a blackbird
    And snapped off her (nose).

oney   queen   bread   maid   guard + n   nose
                                              (garden)

eye
(I)

pussy

coat

LITTLE PUSSY

👁 like little 🐱,
Her 🧥 is 🧺 warm,
And if 👁 don't hurt her
She'll do me no h+🦾;
I'll 🪢 pull her 🐈,
Nor drive her away,
But 👁 and 🐱
Very gently will play.

sew
(so)

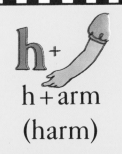
h+arm
(harm)

knot
(not)

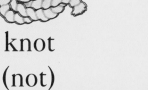

tail

hay
(hey)

cat

fiddle

cow

THE CAT AND THE FIDDLE

, diddle, diddle!
  The 🐱 and the 🎻,
The 🐄 jumped over the 🌙;
  The little 🐶 laughed
2 see such sport,
  And the 🥧 ran away with
the 🥄.

 moon    dog   two (to)    dish    spoon

sheep

wool

eye
(I)

3
three

BAA, BAA, BLACK SHEEP

Baa, baa, black 🐑,
Have you any 〰️?
Yes, marry, have 👁,
3 👝👝👝 full;
One 4 my master,
One 4 my dame,
But none 4 the little 👦
Who 😢 in the lane.

bags

four
(for)

boy

cries

jack
(Jack)

hill

pail

crown

JACK AND JILL

Jack and Jill went up the hill,
2 fetch a bucket of water;
Jack fell down, and broke his crown,
And Jill came tumbling after.
Then Jack got up and off did trot,
As fast as he could caper,
2 old Dame Dob, who patch+ed his knob
With vinegar and brown paper.

two
(to)

patch + ed
(patched)

knob
(nob)

paper

wall

gr + **8**
gr + eight
(great)

HUMPTY DUMPTY

Humpty Dumpty sat on a ,
Humpty Dumpty had a gr+8 fall;
All the 's , and all the
's men
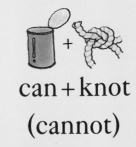 put Humpty Dumpty
together again.

king

horses

can + knot
(cannot)

locks

bee

(be)

knot

(not)

dishes

CURLY-LOCKS

Curly-, Curly-,
  wilt thou  mine?
Thou shalt  wash the ,
  nor yet feed the swine;
But sit on a , and
  a fine seam,
And feed upon , ,
  and .

shion   sew   strawberries   sugar   cream

pig

two
(to)

FIVE TOES

This little 🐷 went **2** market;
This little 🐷 stayed at 🏠;
This little 🐷 had 🍖;
This little 🐷 had none;
This little 🐷 said, "Wee, wee!"
👁 can't find my way 🏠."

home

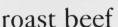
roast beef

eye

(I)

pudding

pie

girls

GEORGY PORGY

Georgy Porgy,
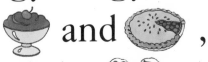 and ,
Kissed the
and made them cr+eye .
When the
came out 2 play,
Georgy Porgy ran away.

cr + eye

(cry)

boys

two

(to)

3
three

mice

C
(see)

THREE BLIND MICE

3 blind 🐭! C how they run!
They all ran after the 👨‍🌾's wife,
Who cut off their 🐱 + s
with a carving 🔪.
Did U ever C such
a thing in your life
As 3 blind 🐭?

rmer

tail
(tails)

knife

U
(you)

horse

two
(to)

lady

rings

BANBURY CROSS

Ride a cock-🐴
2 Banbury Cross,
2 see an old 👸 🐴 upon a white 🐴.
💍💍 on her ✋,
and 🔔 on her 🦶,
She shall have 🎵 wherever she goes.

fingers

bells

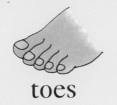
toes

music

cat

eye
(I)

two
(to)

PUSSY-CAT AND QUEEN

"Pussy-🐱, pussy-🐱,
   Where have you been?"
"👁've been 2 London
   2 look at the 👸."
"Pussy-🐱, pussy-🐱,
   What did you there?"
"👁 frightened a little 🐭
   Under the 🪑."

queen

mouse

chair

baby

tree

top

HUSH-A-BYE

Hush-a-bye, 🍼 ,
on the 🌳🪀 !
When the ☁️ blows
the 🛏️ will 🪨 ;
When the bough **b**⁺🧹
the 🛏️ will fall;
Down will come 🍼 ,
bough, 🛏️ and all.

wind

cradle

rock

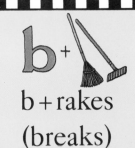
b+rakes
(breaks)

eye
(I)

hen

dishes

house

THE CLEVER HEN

👁 had a little 🐔 , the prettiest
  ever seen,
She washed me the 🏺🍽 and
  kept the 🏠 clean;
She went to the 🏭 to fetch me
  some 🧂 ,
She brought it home in less than
  an hour;
She baked me my 🍞 , she
  brewed me my ale,
She sat by the 🔥 and told
  many a fine 🐈 .

| mill | flour | bread | fire | tail (tale) |

horses

turnips

watches

eye

(I)

IF WISHES WERE HORSES

If wishes were ,
    beggars would ride.
If 🍃 were 🕰,
    👁 would wear **1** by my side.
And if "ifs" and "ands"
    Were 🍲 and 🍳,
There'd 🐝 no work **4** tinkers!

1   🍲   🍳   🐝   **4**
one   pots   pans   bee   four
                                    (be)   (for)

bees

hay

BEES

A swarm of 🐝 in May
Is worth a load of 🟫;
A swarm of 🐝 in June
Is worth a silver 🥄;
A swarm of 🐝 in July
Is 🪢 worth a 🪰.

spoon

knot
(not)

fly

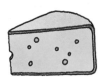